Contents

1 Triangle of Fear

A triangle of fear?
Why should you fear a triangle?

What sort of story is this?
It is a story of mystery.
It is a story of strange things.
It is a story of things that disappear.

Things disappear.
What things?
Planes, ships and people
have all disappeared.
They all disappeared in an area
near Florida in America.
An area the shape of a triangle.

The triangle stretches between
the Florida coast, the Bahamas and Bermuda.
It is called the Bermuda Triangle.

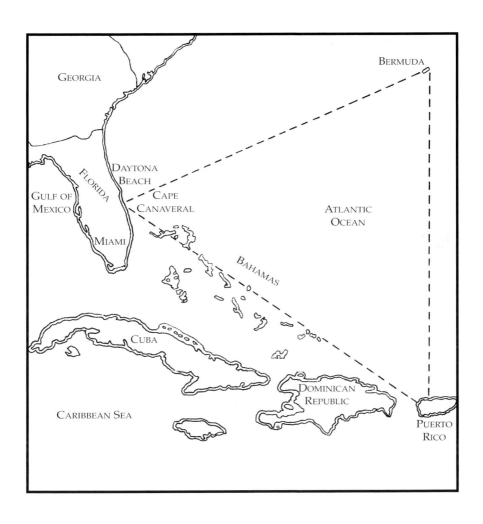

2 Missing

How can planes, ships and people
just disappear?
It is a fact that some
have never been seen again.

A plane with 32 people on board went into
the triangle and disappeared.
A ship with 12 people went into the triangle
and was never seen again.
Another plane with 20 people
went into the triangle and vanished.

Five planes flying together
went into the triangle.
They were never seen again.
A rescue plane was sent after them.
It had 13 people on board.
It, too, disappeared.

AMAZING STORIES

Scientifiction
Stories by

A. Hyatt Verrill
John W. Campbell, Jr.
Edmond Hamilton

Tales about the Bermuda Triangle have always interested people.

Would you travel through this triangle?
Many people won't.

A triangle of fear.
Some call it the Triangle of Death.

What is happening?
There are many different stories and ideas.
See what you think.

3 Flight 19

Let's follow the journey of the five planes.

It was December 1945.
It was a training flight.
All the pilots were students.
The leader was a trained pilot.
They were called Flight 19.

Their mission was to fly 160 miles east.
Then 40 miles north.
Then fly west back to their base.

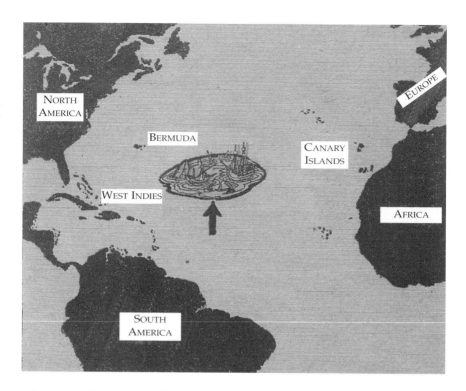

The area already had a sinister reputation even before the triangle was invented – wrecks were thought to end up in the Sargasso Sea.

All the pilots got ready for take off.
All except one.

One man did not go.
He did not want to fly that day.
He said that he had a feeling
that something was wrong.

It was a clear day in December.
Flight 19 took off.
The take off went well.
Everything seemed fine.

Then, soon afterwards the leader
contacted the control tower.

The message went something like this:

Leader: Control Tower.
This is Flight 19.

Control: Go ahead Flight 19.
This is Control.

Leader: Control, this is an emergency.
We seem to be off course.
We cannot see land.
Repeat, we cannot see land.

Control: Flight 19.
What is your position?

Leader: We are not sure.
We seem to be lost.
We don't know where we are.

Control: Flight 19.
This is Control.
Head due west.

Leader: Control.
Which way is west?
We don't know which way to go.
Everything is wrong.
Everything is strange.
We can't be sure of anything.
Even the sea looks strange.

Control:	Flight 19.
	This is Control.
	What is your position?
Leader:	We must be about 225 miles
	north-east of base.
	It looks like we are …

That was the last that was heard
from Flight 19.
There were 14 men flying that day.
Nothing was heard from them again.
There was only silence.

4 The Search

A rescue plane was sent out at once.
There were 13 men on this plane.

It flew to where they thought
Flight 19 had been.
It flew into the triangle.
Nothing was heard from any of the men again.
There was only silence.
The rescue plane had also gone missing.

Lots of boats and planes joined the search.
They saw nothing.
They heard nothing.
They found nothing.

What had happened?

5 What People Think

Could it have been a UFO?
Some people think that UFOs
fly around the triangle.
They catch planes and ships.
Maybe they take them to another planet.

Some people think that aliens
have an underwater base in the triangle.
The aliens destroy anything
moving near their base.

Could it be some strange force
pulling things into the sea?
Some people think that it is.
Maybe planes and ships are pulled
into another world.
Maybe they are pulled through time.

One man believes that the disappearances
are caused by giant gas bubbles.
He thinks that the gas builds up underwater
and comes to the surface
in apple-sized bubbles.
When the bubbles burst the gas is released.
The gas could catch fire and explode
if it came into contact with hot engines.

One idea is that a lost city
lies under the sea.
It is known as the Lost City of Atlantis.
The city was supposed to use crystals
to provide its power.
The crystals may still be
at the bottom of the sea.
They may be sending out rays that confuse
the instruments on planes and ships
so they don't know where they are.

6 Strange Goings On

Is it that planes and ships really do get lost?
Perhaps they do not know where they are
and in the end they sink into the sea.

It is true that there is something odd
about the Bermuda Triangle.
Sailors and pilots use a compass
to tell them where they are.
The compass usually points towards
magnetic north rather than true north.
As sailors and pilots travel around the earth
they have to work out the difference
between magnetic north and true north
so that they know where they are.

There are only two places on earth
where magnetic north and true north
become confused.
One is near the east coast of Japan.
Japanese fishermen call it the Devil's Sea.
It is known for its strange disappearances.
The other is the Bermuda Triangle.

Some people think that Flight 19 got lost.
The men were not very good pilots.
They were still in training.

Their leader did not know the area very well.
We know that he was lost.
Maybe all the planes flew around in circles.
They didn't know where they were going.
They flew around for a long time.
The planes ran out of fuel.
They fell into the sea,
filled with water and sank.

What about the rescue plane?
Well, it was dark when it took off.
Some people said that there was an explosion.
They think that there was a fire on the plane.

Some oil was seen on the water
where the rescue plane went down.
The weather was too bad to look
for anything else.

7 No Clues

Nothing has ever been found.
There have never been any clues.
No bodies.
No wreckage from the planes or the ships.
Nothing.

There are so many ideas about the triangle.
Could it just be bad weather?
Thunderstorms, high waves,
strong currents or hurricanes?

Is it a mystery?
Or is there an explanation?

The Bermuda Triangle.
Is it really a triangle of death?